THE STORY OF RADIOACTIVITY

By Colin A. Mawson

Illustrations by Marvin Besunder

Prentice-Hall, Inc., Englewood Cliffs, N.J.

The Story of Radioactivity
by Colin A. Mawson

Library of Congress Catalog Card Number: 74-83352

Printed in the United States of America • *J*
13-850289-7

Prentice-Hall International, Inc., *London*
Prentice-Hall of Australia, Pty. Ltd., *Sydney*
Prentice-Hall of Canada, Ltd., *Toronto*
Prentice-Hall of India Private Ltd., *New Delhi*
Prentice-Hall of Japan, Inc., *Tokyo*

CONTENTS

1

What Is Radioactivity?

Most people seem to be afraid of radioactivity. There are many reasons, but one of them is that the first time the world heard much about radioactivity was when the atom bombs went off in Japan.

Another reason is that people know that too much radiation can be harmful. You cannot see radioactivity. You cannot feel it, hear it, or taste it, so it seems to be something mysterious that you cannot avoid. People are often afraid of the unknown, but it usually turns out that when you have learned something about it, it is far less frightening. It may even be very useful.

One of the reasons that the Spaniards conquered South America so easily was that the Indians were frightened by their horses—but, once the Indians recovered from their fear, it didn't take them long to find out how useful horses could be.

Man has always been surrounded by radiation, and has always used some kind of radiation. Light and heat, X-rays and radio waves are all different kinds of radiation. Light is not frightening, but if you have too much of it on a sunny day at the beach you will get a painful sunburn. Heat is fine in the right place, but it can be deadly in a burning house or out in the desert.

The kinds of radiation that we call radioactivity can be dangerous if we do not take sensible precautions. But if we understand them, and use our knowledge properly, they can make our lives richer without doing us any harm.

Radioactive substances give off energy all the time. Ordinary sources of energy are usually hot (a fire), under high pressure (a boiler), or travelling fast (a bullet). Radioactivity comes from changes right inside atoms—changes which are not affected by heat or pressure or speed.

The various forms of energy given off by radioactive substances have the names of the first three letters of the Greek alphabet: α (alpha), β (beta) and γ (gamma). An alpha particle is rather heavy and each one carries with it a lot of energy, so if it hits something it can do a lot of damage. It is like a bullet, except that it cannot penetrate very far. An alpha particle can be stopped by a sheet of paper and it gives up all its energy in a very small distance. That is why it is so destructive. An example of this principle would also be: If you were to stop a car in 200 yards the brakes would only be warm, but if you stop it in 20 yards, they may be burned out.

Many radioactive substances give off beta particles. β particles have various different energies,

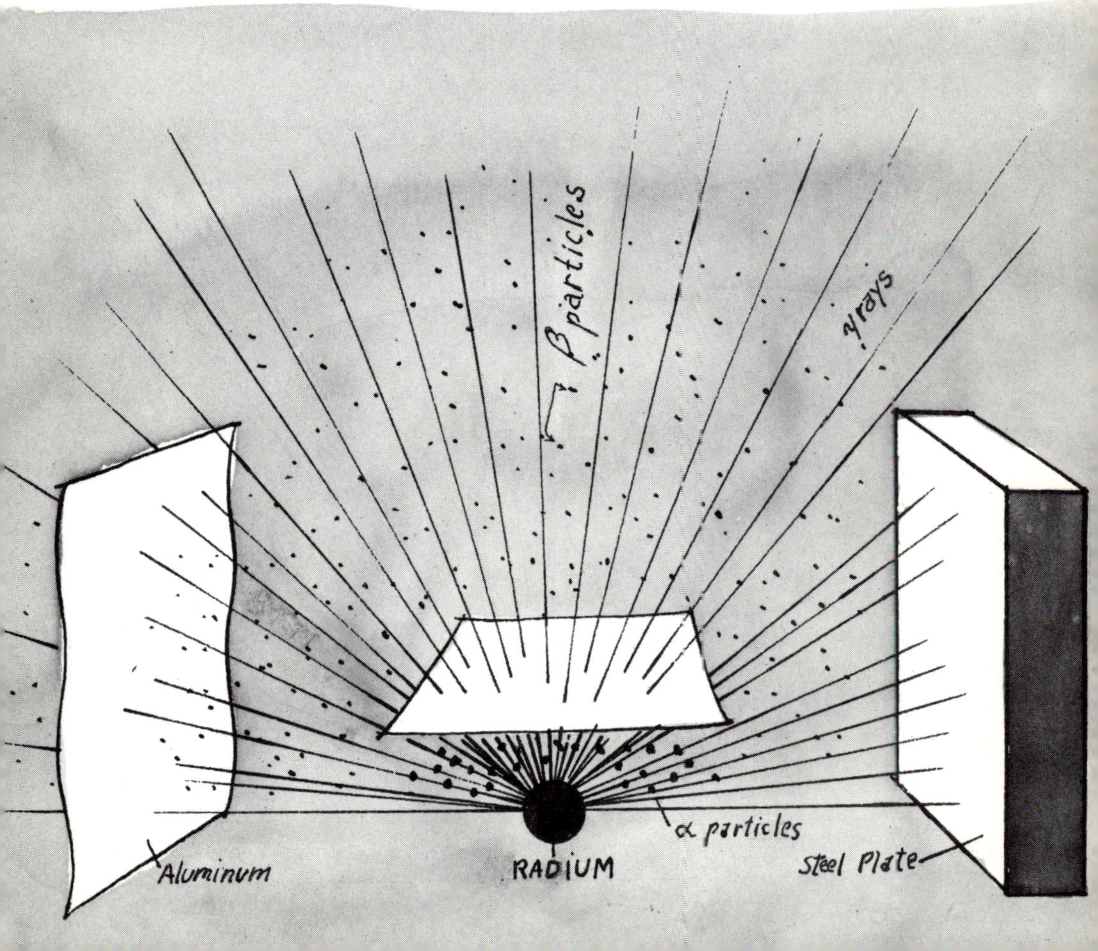

but most of them can be stopped by a few thicknesses of aluminum foil. Gamma rays often come from the same substances as β particles. They are very much like X-rays, and most of them can penetrate a brick wall quite easily. Some can even pass through several inches of steel plate.

All these kinds of radiation are around us all the time, and always have been, in small quantities. There are very small amounts of RADIUM in all soils and rocks, and delicate instruments like GEIGER COUNTERS can detect this radiation.

We are not only surrounded by radiation, but our own bodies actually contain a radioactive element, potassium. There are three natural kinds —ISOTOPES—of potassium, and one of them is radioactive. There isn't much, but it does give off β particles and γ rays.

We get along quite well with the α, β and γ radiation that comes from our natural surroundings and more powerful forms of radiation—the cosmic rays—that come in from outer space. Cosmic rays can even penetrate deep mines.

Why don't we worry about this natural radioactivity? Well, for one thing we cannot do anything about it, and the human race has survived pretty well up to now. But the main reason is that the amount of natural radiation is very small.

We know now that we can live with much larger amounts of radiation if we make sure that the amount of radiation that we actually *receive* remains very small. We must know how to protect ourselves—just as a fireman puts on an asbestos suit or a person wears special glasses under a sun lamp.

2

How It Started

The history of our knowledge of radioactivity gives a good idea of how researchers work. Most people have seen events that are new to science, but very few are clever enough to realize that they *are* new.

In 1895 Wilhelm Roentgen discovered X-RAYS. This made people interested in any kind of invisible rays. A year later Henri Becquerel was repeating some experiments that Niepce de St. Victor had done before in 1867.

Henri Becquerel knew that some uranium compounds became PHOSPHORESCENT after they had been exposed to X-rays. He wanted to know if they would emit PENETRATING RAYS after exposure to ordinary light. Here is Becquerel's question:

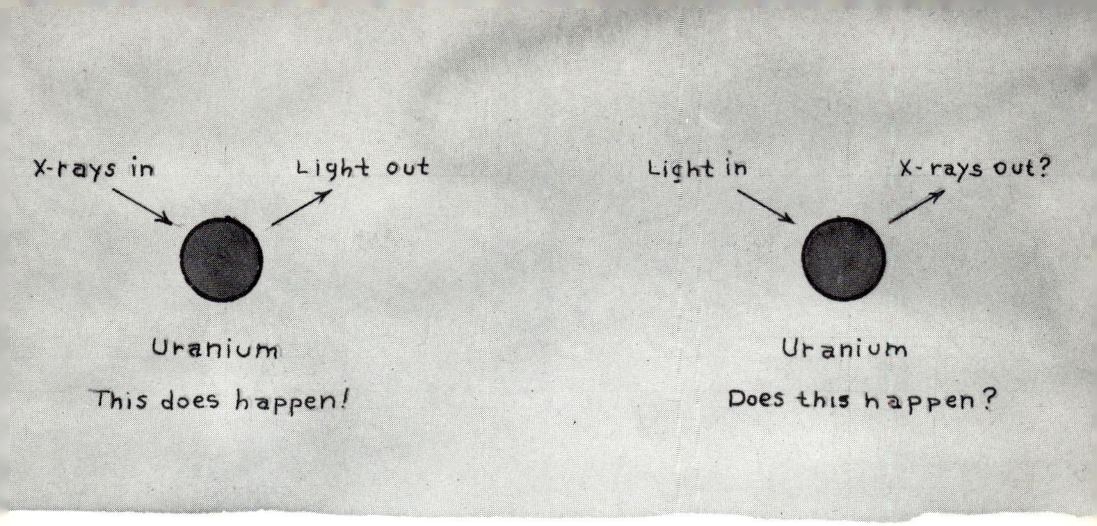

Becquerel had a uranium compound that he kept in a drawer. By accident, it was put on top of a new photographic plate that was wrapped in black paper. The uranium had *not* been exposed to light, but when the plate was developed it was fogged at just the place where the uranium had been.

Instead of saying "Too bad!" and throwing the plate away, Becquerel saw that he had made a new discovery. He had expected to find just such rays coming from uranium *after* illumination with ordinary light. Now he found that uranium emits penetrating radiations whether it has been exposed to light or not.

Within two years these first experiments led to a lot more research. Becquerel found that the air around uranium became electrified, and that the

"radioactivity" (as he called the new rays) was not affected by heat or cold. Ordinary chemical reactions *are* affected by heat—most of them go faster when the temperature is raised. Some chemical reactions electrify the air around them (a piece of glowing phosphorus and a burning match are examples) but uranium is different.

If you put a piece of uranium inside a thin glass tube, pump out all the air, and seal the tube, the air *outside* the tube will be electrified (or IONIZED, as we call it today). It is not a matter of air or moisture affecting the uranium. Something is constantly coming out of the uranium, and whatever we do to the uranium it continues to come out.

This last point is very important. The radioactivity goes on and on. So far as Becquerel could tell, the uranium did not change—it was not being burned up. It seemed to be able to keep on shooting out energy indefinitely.

3

Knowledge Explosion

Before scientists can get far with a problem they have to make measurements, and the blackening of a photographic plate was not good enough. Becquerel soon found that the electroscope was a much better instrument. The electroscope works on the principle that bodies with the same kind of electric charge repel one another. It is a box containing an insulated metal rod with a piece of gold foil attached at its top end. When the battery is connected, the rod becomes electrically charged. Because the rod and the gold foil have the same kind of charge, the foil flies away from the rod, and stays there. The bigger the charge on the rod, the larger the angle will be between the rod and the gold foil. When the battery is switched off, the foil remains up for a long time.

Becquerel found that if he put a little uranium in the box or near the knob on the rod, the gold foil

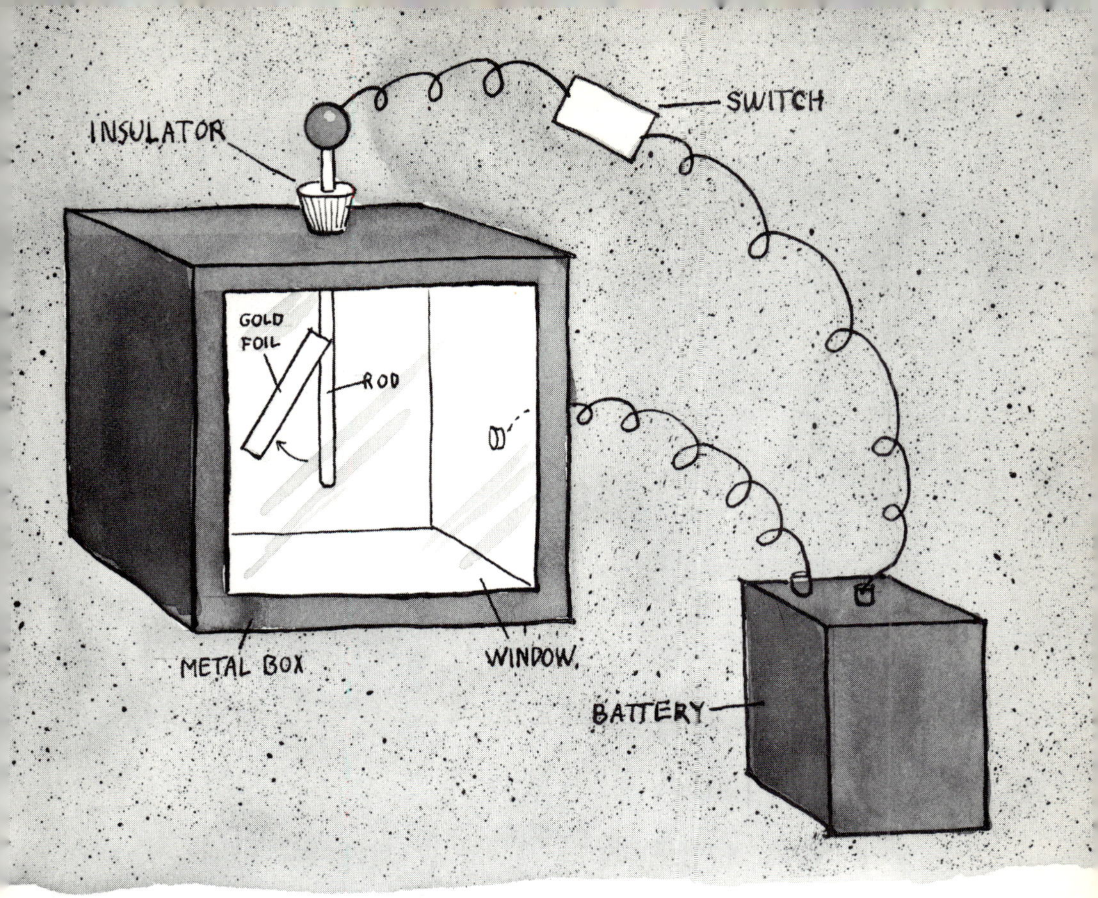

fell very quickly—the electroscope was discharged. The rays from the uranium were not spoiling the insulation—they were electrifying the air. It acted as a CONDUCTOR of electricity so that the charge could leak away from the rod. The rate of the leak, measured by the rate of fall of the gold foil, was a measure of the amount of radioactivity.

DISCOVERY OF RADIUM

Soon after Becquerel's discovery of radioactivity, Marie Curie decided to find out whether any

other substances were radioactive. She was not a paid research worker, but her husband Pierre worked in the School of Physics and Chemistry in Paris and he let her use a corner of his storeroom for her experiments.

Marie Curie examined almost every known element, but in the end there were only two that were radioactive—uranium and thorium. However, she noticed a very strange fact—a uranium *ore*, pitchblende, was much more radioactive than uranium *metal!*

Madame Curie decided that there must be some unknown element in the pitchblende that was more radioactive than uranium, and she set about trying to separate it from the ore. She used methods similar to those taught in school today for analysis of mixtures of chemicals. She obtained products much more radioactive than pitchblende, and she soon found that she had *two* new radioactive substances. One, which she called polonium in honor of her native Poland, came out along with BISMUTH. The other, which separated with BARIUM, she called radium, because her preparation was 900 times as radioactive as uranium.

The Curies knew from Marie's experiments that radium remained in the wastes left behind in refining uranium from pitchblende, so they started work on about a ton of these residues. By repeated crystallizations and recrystallizations, they separated the radium from the barium and ended up with one tenth of a GRAM of pure radium, over a million times more radioactive than uranium!

This wonderful and heroic piece of chemistry took only four years. It is one of the noblest feats of science. The product startled scientists all over the world and led to a tremendous outburst of research.

4

The Radium Mystery

Radium glowed in the dark because its intense radioactivity ionized the air around it. Radium salts were distinctly warmer than their surroundings—obviously they were giving off energy, but where was the energy coming from? Everything around a radium salt—the container, the bench top, even the air—became radioactive too.* These, and many other strange observations, had to be explained. It was still only 1902.

Ernest Rutherford and Frederick Soddy, working in Montreal, had solved many of the problems by 1903. They found that radium continually gives off a radioactive gas called radon. The radioactivity of radon gradually decreases—half of it

* The Curies called this "induced" radioactivity.

is gone in four days—but as it DECAYS the radon deposits a radioactive *solid,* which settles out on surrounding surfaces. This solid is the reason for the "induced" radioactivity noticed by the Curies. It also decays—half disappears in three minutes. These "decay products" are only the beginning of a long chain of radioactive elements, ending up with non-radioactive lead.

To see why radium seemed so mysterious in 1902 we need to understand what scientists believed about the atom at that time.

DALTON'S ATOM

Some time between 1801 and 1803 John Dalton proposed that every element consists of very small "atoms." The atoms of a particular element are alike, and different from those of all other elements. Compounds consist of two or more elements grouped together in the form of molecules—for example a water molecule contains two hydrogen atoms and one oxygen atom.

Dalton thought that if you cut a lump of iron in two, then cut one of the pieces in two, and went on cutting, you would end up with a tiny bit of iron that you could no longer cut in two. That would be an iron atom. He believed that it might be impossible to break any atom apart.

RADIOACTIVE ATOMS

When Rutherford was studying the radioactivity of thorium the results of his experiments were strangely variable. One of his students, Owens, showed that due to air currents, the thorium was giving off a radioactive gas. If this gas was blown away, the radioactivity decreased. The gas was certainly not thorium, so somehow thorium must be changing into a different element, which was named thoron.

In 1903 Soddy, working with Sir William Ramsay, found that radium compounds always

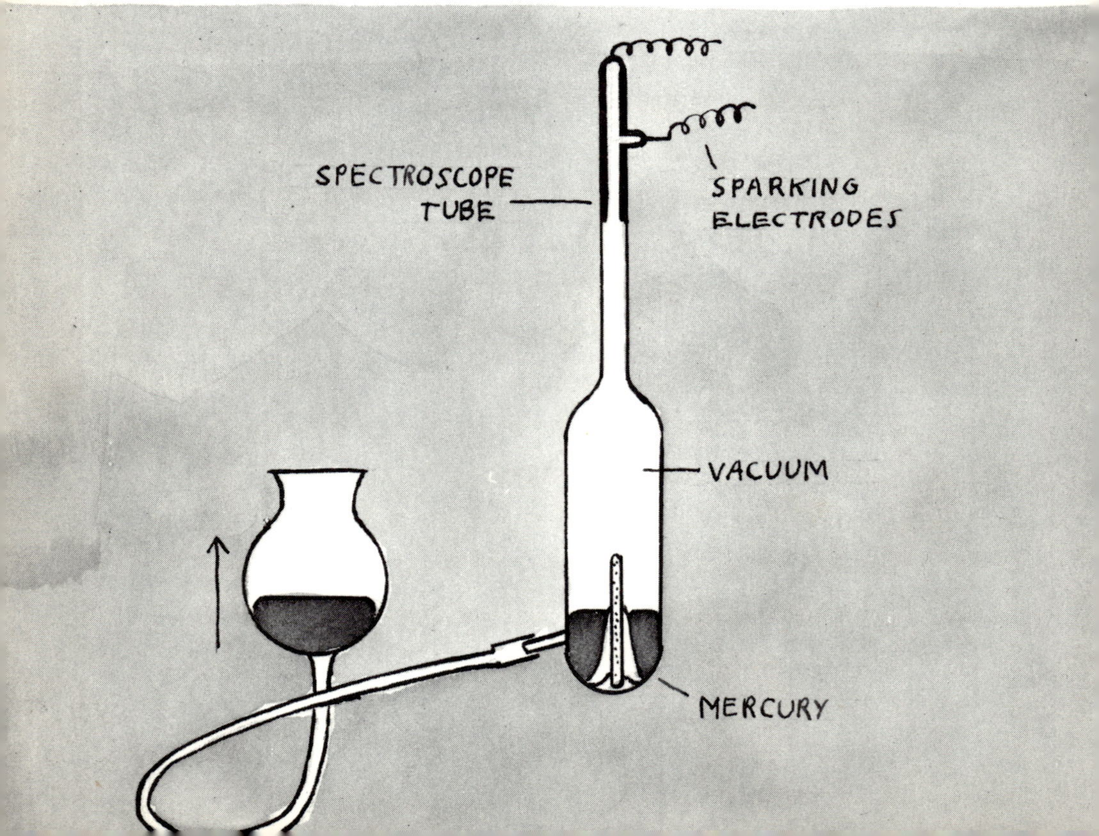

contain some HELIUM, a well-known gas sometimes found in oil wells. They suggested that helium must be one of the decay products of radium. This was finally proved by sealing some radon in a very thin glass tube inside an apparatus made so that any gas appearing *outside* the thin tube could be collected. The glass was thin enough to allow the α particles from the radon to pass through, but no gas could get out. After leaving the apparatus for six days, a gas was found outside the thin tube that turned out to be helium. The α particles seemed to have changed into helium!

Here was something new and exciting. Not only could thorium change into thoron and radium into radon, but α particles were not just rays—they actually became helium. They passed through the glass tube because they had so much energy—much more than the atoms of an ordinary gas.

This work proved that some atoms *could* break apart, that the radioactivity of radium was caused by breaking apart of its atoms, and that one of these parts was helium. The other broken part then went on breaking up to form the long chain of radioactive elements that ends as lead.

Scientists soon found they were faced with another mystery that seemed to destroy one of their firmest beliefs. Radium and all radium compounds are about 1.5 degrees warmer than their surroundings. They believed that energy could not be created, but radium was continually giving out energy—energy seemed to be coming from nowhere, continuously!

A temperature rise of 1.5 degrees does not seem much, but the average life of a radium atom is about 2,300 years, so the generation of heat goes on for a long time. In fact, by the time one ounce of radium has decayed away, it has given out as much heat as the burning of 30 *tons* of coal!

By 1903 Rutherford had solved the mystery of where the energy came from. He had shown that radioactivity was due to the breaking-up of radioactive atoms. In the case of radium he felt sure that the bit that came out was an α particle, and that this was a positively charged helium atom. He suggested that the NUCLEUS of the atom contained positively charged particles all held tightly together in a very small space. Positive charges repel one another, so to hold them closely together requires a lot of energy. When one of them breaks away, part of that energy is no longer needed, so it is carried away with the α particle and *appears as heat* as soon as the α particle hits something and stops moving. So the answer was that a great deal of energy is bound up inside the atom and when the atom breaks up the energy is released.

When a narrow beam of α particles is shot at a thin sheet of foil, most of them go straight through, but a few change direction. Rutherford explained this by showing that when an α particle hits the nucleus of an atom it bounces off like a billiard ball. Most of the space inside an atom is empty, but in the middle there is a tiny nucleus carrying a positive electric charge. The amount of the charge depends on the weight of the nucleus. Around the nucleus is a cloud of ELECTRONS, circulating like planets round the sun.

5

Neutrons

Until 1919 the only radioactive elements known were those that occur in nature—uranium, thorium, actinium and their decay products (such as radium, radon, polonium, and thoron) and radioactive isotopes of potassium and rubidium. Scientists knew that if they wanted to make some ordinary element radioactive they would have to do something violent to the nucleus—chip a particle out or push a particle in. The particle would have to hit the nucleus with tremendous force.

Rutherford had the very sort of energetic "bullet" that was needed—the α particle. When he shot α particles into nitrogen he observed not only the positively charged nitrogen atoms, which he had expected, but also some positively charged *hydrogen* atoms, which he had not expected.

Rutherford knew that there was no hydrogen in his nitrogen to start with, so it must have been produced by α particles hitting nitrogen atoms. It turned out that oxygen was also produced in this reaction: when an α particle hits a nitrogen atom it produces a PROTON (a positively charged hydrogen atom) *and* an oxygen atom. This was the first time man had carried out an artificial "nuclear reaction" or TRANSMUTATION.

The next part of the story seemed very mysterious at the time. Two German workers, Walther Bothe and H. Becker, were bombarding a foil made of beryllium, a light metal rather like magnesium, with α particles from radium. They detected a very penetrating radiation that went through several inches of lead. Marie Curie's daughter, Irène, working with her husband, tried the same experiment two years later with aluminum foil and they too noticed the powerful radiation. However, they also found that they could extract some radioactive material from the foil. It was not aluminum—it was radioactive *phosphorus!* This was the first RADIOACTIVE ISOTOPE produced artificially.

The only reasonable explanation for this surprising result was that when an α particle hits an aluminum nucleus, the aluminum changes into radioactive phosphorus. The trouble is that if you add up the weight of the α particle and the aluminum atom, it does not equal the weight of the phosphorus atom, which is one unit of weight too light. Could it be that the missing weight was some brand-new particle? And was this new particle the "penetrating radiation" that people had been puzzling about?

Another discovery about the "penetrating radiation" seemed almost ridiculous at the time. Although the radiation would go through several inches of lead it was stopped by paraffin wax or water. Now the efficiency of a RADIATION SHIELD depends on its DENSITY. A very dense substance like lead is usually a much better shield than a light substance like wax, but this kind of radiation was stopped by wax and went right through lead.

Several people had suggested before that a particle should exist that was very energetic, had no electrical charge, and had a mass about equal to the hydrogen atom. They had all looked for it, but none had detected it. Finally, the new radiation was explained by Sir James Chadwick.

The answer was found with the CLOUD CHAMBER invented by C.T.R. Wilson. This is a very beautiful device which shows up the tracks of charged particles as they pass through a saturated vapor. The penetrating radiation was not charged, so it made no tracks, but when it hit an atomic nucleus, charged particles were produced, and tracks at once appeared.

A beam of "penetrating radiation" was shot into a cloud chamber containing nitrogen. Tracks appeared, and each was a V—one leg of the V was thin and the other was thick. Chadwick recognized the thin ones as α particle tracks and the thick ones as tracks produced by charged boron, an element found in borax and boric acid. What

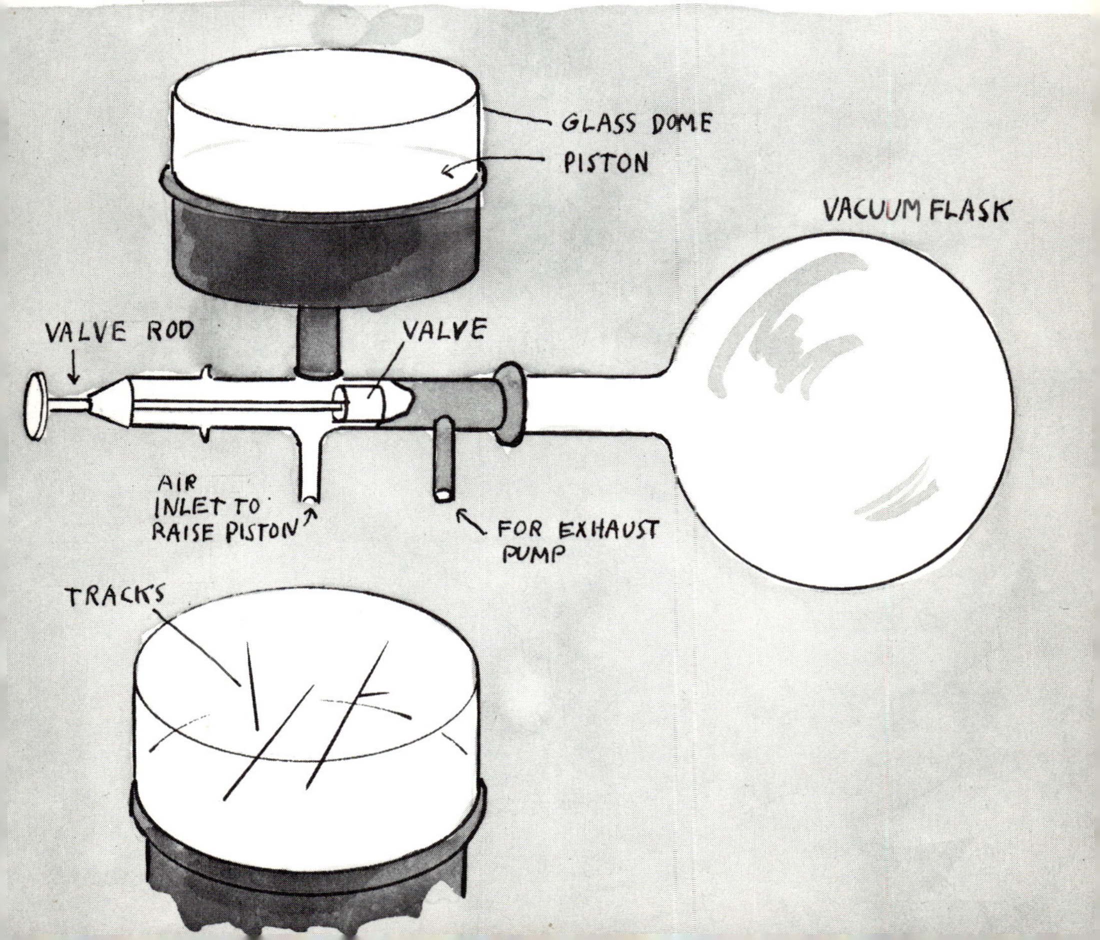

had happened was that something uncharged (because it made no track) had hit a nitrogen atom and broken the nucleus into a boron nucleus and an α particle. To do this it had to have weight, so the "something" had to be an uncharged particle. Chadwick called it a "neutron."

The discovery of the neutron was a tremendous event. Using streams of neutrons it should be possible to produce radioactive forms of almost any element.

Until the neutron was discovered the atomic nucleus had been supposed to consist of protons and electrons. Now it became clear that it is built up from protons and *neutrons*, and this is really the most important result of Chadwick's work.

6

Artificial Radioactivity

When the news of the discovery of the neutron reached Rome, Enrico Fermi decided to try bombarding a great many elements with neutrons to see if he could produce radioactive elements. He bombarded fluorine gas with neutrons and obtained radioactive FLUORINE. The radioactive fluorine decayed rapidly (half of it disappeared in 11 seconds) and to detect it he had to run all the way down the corridor from the laboratory to the counting room!

Later that year Fermi made a big discovery. He was irradiating silver with neutrons to produce radioactive silver, and he found that much more radioactive silver was formed if the neutron source was under water or buried in a lump of paraffin wax.

COUNTING ROOM
E. FERMI

Fermi explained this by saying that the neutrons coming out of his BERYLLIUM-RADON SOURCE were travelling so fast that they often shot right past a silver nucleus without entering it. If they were *slowed down* they were much more likely to break in, rather than just glancing off. The water or the wax slowed the neutrons down because they hit a great many hydrogen atoms on their way through, slowing down a little (losing energy) at each collision.

This slowing-down effect is called "moderation" and the water or wax is a MODERATOR. As we shall see later, the moderator is a vital part of most kinds of atomic reactors.

Equipped with neutron sources and moderators many workers were soon able to produce radioactive forms of most of the known elements. Emilio Segrè even produced an element which he called technetium, that was not only radioactive but had never been found on earth before!

7

The Fission Mystery

When Fermi irradiated uranium and thorium with neutrons he expected to obtain radioactive uranium and thorium. However, the products did not behave chemically as they should. When Irène Joliot-Curie repeated Fermi's experiments she separated a radioactive element that behaved just like lanthanum (one of the RARE EARTH metals). Ida Noddack wrote in 1934 that "the nuclei might break into a number of large pieces which would no doubt be isotopes of known elements" but nobody took her suggestion seriously for nearly five years.

Otto Hahn and Fritz Strassmann, in Germany, were also irradiating uranium with neutrons. They too kept finding something that behaved chemically like lanthanum. They added some genuine lanthanum and separated it again in a very pure form. To their surprise the radioactivity came out along wth the lanthanum. Not only that, but if they added ordinary barium to the radioactive mixture obtained by bombarding uranium with neutrons, and then separated the barium, the barium was radioactive!

Hahn and Strassmann were forced, much against their will, to conclude that the neutron bombardment had changed uranium into lanthanum and barium. They rushed their discovery into print in the English journal *Nature* in January 1939. They sent a copy of the paper to their friend Lise Meitner, a German refugee in Copenhagen. Lise was staying for Christmas with her nephew, Otto Frisch, and they spent the holidays discussing these extraordinary results. In February they published a paper in *Nature* stating quite plainly that uranium had been split by the neutrons, explaining how this could happen, and giving the process the name of "fission."

Niels Bohr had suggested what happens inside the nucleus of an atom when a particle enters it. The protons and neutrons inside the nucleus are so closely packed that it behaves rather like a drop of liquid. The new particle stirs up the "drop" and the particles inside swirl around until one of them

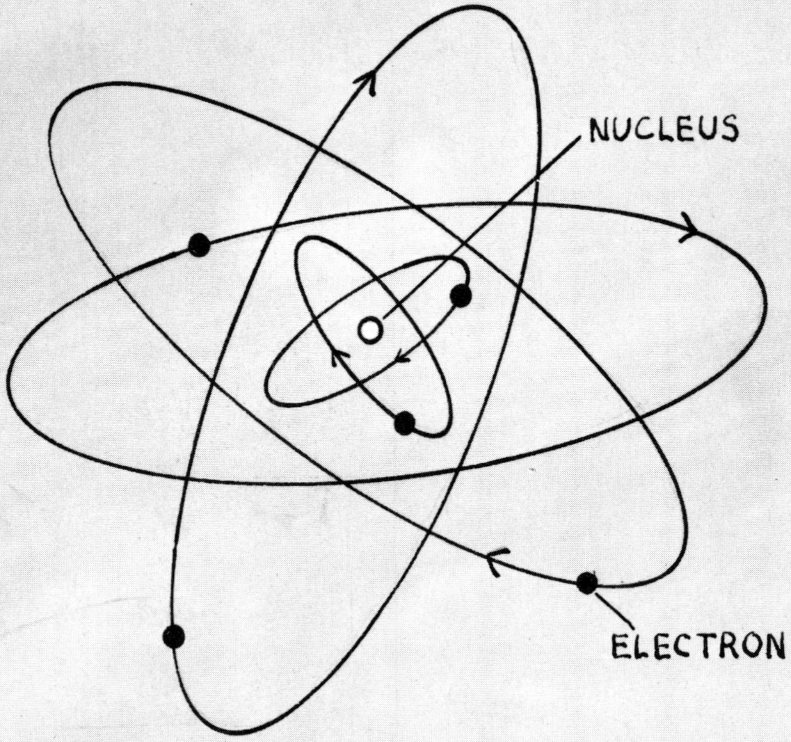
NUCLEUS
ELECTRON

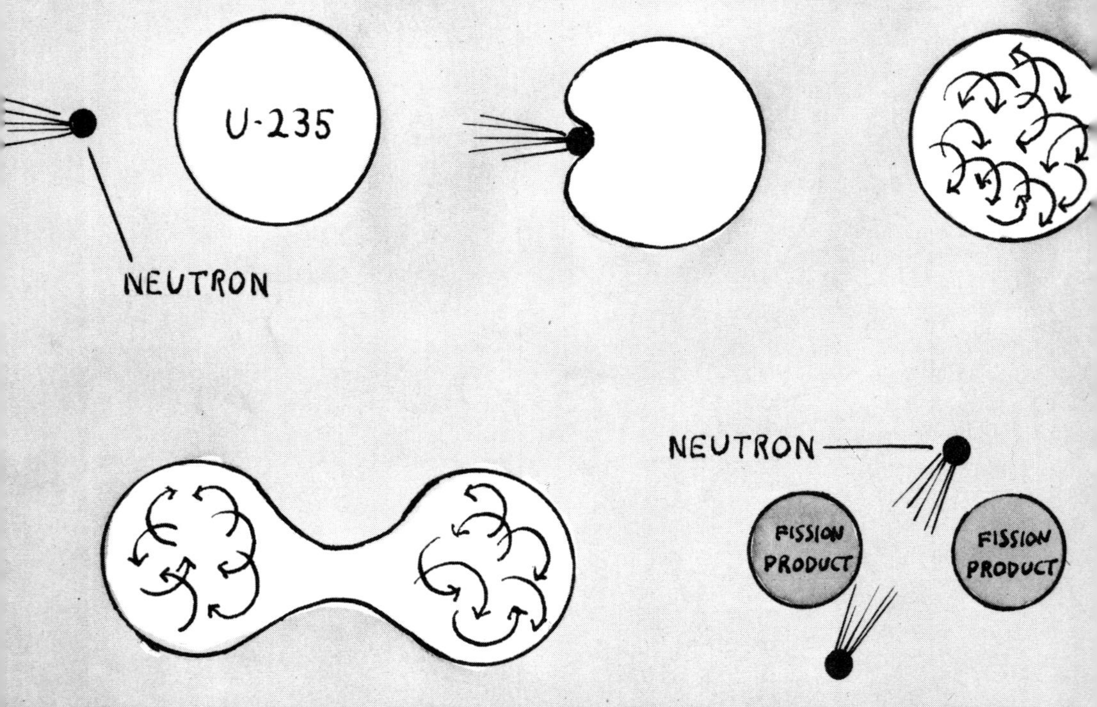
U-235
NEUTRON
NEUTRON
FISSION PRODUCT
FISSION PRODUCT

breaks away and the drop calms down again. The "break-away particle" is radiation. Meitner and Frisch proposed that when a neutron enters a uranium nucleus it is so agitated that it becomes dumb-bell shaped and finally splits at the "waist" into two fairly equal parts. These parts are called fission products, and they are nearly all radioactive.

8

The Chain Reaction

The discovery of fission set off another "knowledge explosion"—about 100 papers appeared on the subject in the first year! The excitement was due to the fact that a new source of energy had been presented to mankind.

When radium decays it emits a large amount of heat, but this is such a slow process that it is not a practical source of power. However, people soon saw that fission was a very different matter.

Albert Einstein had shown that if matter was completely destroyed energy would be produced in its place. The destruction of a very little matter produces a very large amount of heat. When fission occurs in a uranium atom the products weigh just a little less than the uranium atom. The disappearance of matter is only about one part in a thousand, but the energy produced is so enormous that this is the "secret" of the atomic bomb!

Another interesting point about fission is that when one neutron is used up in splitting the uranium atom, *two new neutrons* appear among the products of the reaction. Each of these neutrons could split another uranium atom, producing *four* new neutrons. The next time around we should have eight, the next time sixteen, and so on. This is called a *chain reaction.*

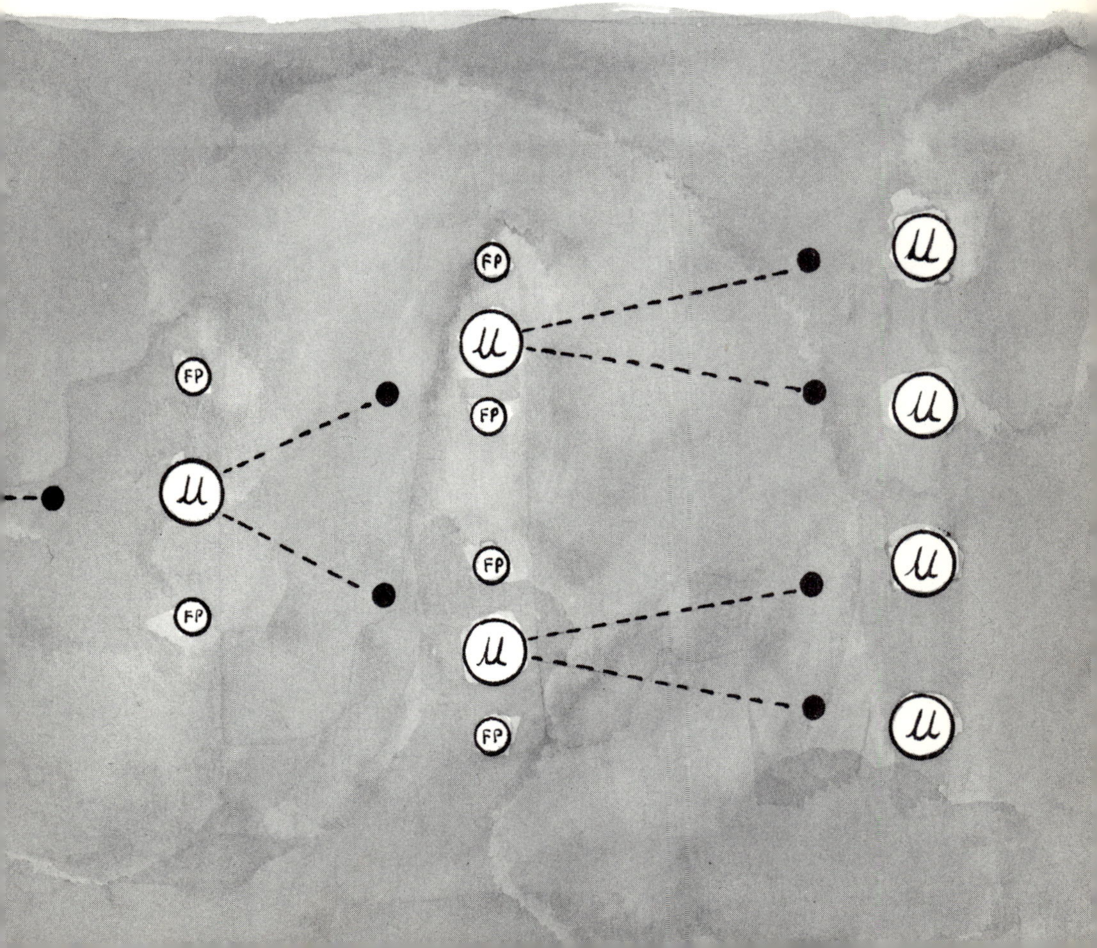

Once the chain reaction starts it looks as if it should keep going until all the uranium is burned up—or until some neutron-absorber is added to break the multiplying chain of neutrons.

Some of the neutrons will be lost by shooting out of the piece of uranium, without hitting any nuclei. A neutron can shoot through a great many uranium atoms without coming anywhere near a uranium nucleus. However, it is possible to reflect the lost neutrons back into the uranium by surrounding it with GRAPHITE, beryllium or several other substances.

A fast neutron may bounce off many nuclei before it penetrates one of them. To make the process efficient neutrons must be slowed down by the use of a moderator. You will remember that this was discovered by Fermi when he was working on radioactive silver.

By the time scientists had discovered what you have read in this chapter they knew that it should be possible to build a *nuclear power reactor* or an atomic bomb. Most of the rest was up to the engineers.

9

The Atomic Pile

Before World War II broke out in September 1939, scientists could see that the fission of uranium might be the source of enormous power. Natural uranium consists mostly of uranium-238, which is not "fissionable." Less than one percent is uranium-235, but it is this isotope that produces energy from the fission reaction. If this power could all be generated very quickly, the device would explode with such force that it would be a terribly efficient bomb. Most scientists at that time were interested mainly in the generation of electric power but the military were soon looking at the possibilities for weapon production.

The basic discoveries in uranium fission had been made in Germany and Italy, but many of their best scientists fled to the United States,

Britain and France for political reasons before the outbreak of war. The collaboration of American, British, French and Canadian scientists, aided by these refugees, combined with the enormous wealth and productivity of the United States, saved the world from the disaster of an atomic bomb in the hands of Hitler and Mussolini.

Fermi went from Rome to Columbia University, where he set to work to convert his laboratory experiments into a large-scale power producing machine. This was no simple matter because many practical difficulties appeared. Most of them were concerned with how "new" neutrons can be "lost" from the chain reaction.

To keep the fission process going we must have at least one new neutron left over to enter the *next uranium-235 nucleus.* If we start with neutrons entering 100 uranium nuclei and causing fission, 200 new neutrons will come out. If, say, 120 of these neutrons are lost, the remaining 80 neutrons will enter nuclei and produce 160 new neutrons. Then 96 of these will be lost, leaving 64 to enter uranium nuclei, producing 128 new neutrons. So first of all we have 200 new neutrons, then 160, next time 128, and so on until very soon hardly any new neutrons will appear and the chain will stop.

There are many ways besides "escape" for neutrons to be lost. Neutrons are absorbed by most elements, producing radioactive isotopes. This will happen to fission neutrons too. They are absorbed in any impurities in the uranium or the moderator, in the walls of the vessel and in the CLADDING around the uranium. Another important "trap" for neutrons is in the uranium itself. Uranium-238 absorbs moderated neutrons, but emits no new neutrons.

These are only some of the ways that new neutrons can be lost to the chain reaction system, and they add up to such a serious total that for some time scientists wondered if it would ever be possible in practice to sustain a real chain reaction.

The only way to find out about this was to try it. Fermi used bars of uranium set in a "pile" of graphite blocks. The graphite was both moderator and reflector. To start the reaction he used the familiar radium-beryllium neutron generator. The pile worked well enough to be encouraging, but for every 10,000 neutrons that entered uranium-235 nuclei, only 8,700 new neutrons survived, so the nuclear reaction was not sustained.

Fermi knew that this was mainly because neutrons were absorbed by impurities in the uranium and the graphite, and he had to wait until the

following year for the chemists to prepare sufficiently pure materials. On December 2, 1942, a Fermi pile operated for the first time with a sustained reaction. It was a near thing—for every 10,000 neutrons causing fission, 10,006 new neutrons were produced.

Fermi's pile, constructed under a Chicago stadium, was not just another laboratory experiment.

It contained 6 tons of uranium metal, 50 tons of uranium oxide, and 400 tons of graphite. It only produced 200 watts of power—enough to light one small room—but it finally answered the question whether man could ever produce power from the fission of uranium.

10

Control of Reactions

When the Chicago reactor achieved a sustained reaction, why did it not go off like a bomb? The chain reaction, once started, multiplies with amazing speed, so one might expect the whole outfit to explode.

To understand this we have to look a little more closely at the design of the pile. The core of the reactor consisted of rods of uranium and uranium oxide surrounded by graphite, which served as moderator and reflector. Inside the core was a rod made of cadmium metal.

Cadmium is a particularly good absorber for neutrons. When the cadmium "control rod" was in the pile it absorbed so many neutrons that the chain reaction could never be sustained. During the "approach to CRITICALITY" the control rod was

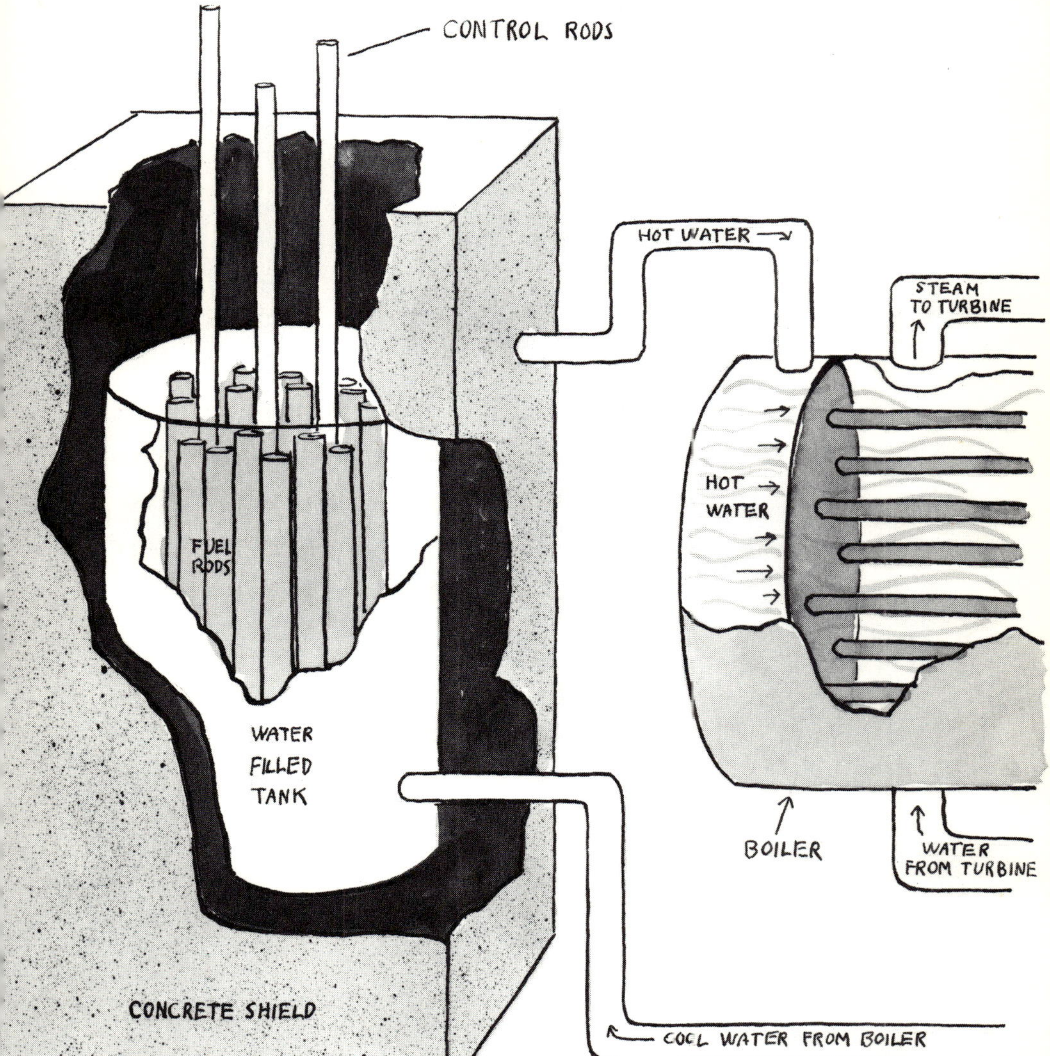
CONTROL RODS
HOT WATER
STEAM TO TURBINE
HOT WATER
FUEL RODS
WATER FILLED TANK
BOILER
WATER FROM TURBINE
CONCRETE SHIELD
COOL WATER FROM BOILER
REACTOR

very slowly pulled out until the point was just reached when the number of new neutrons produced by fission was exactly equal to the number entering uranium-235 nuclei. At this point the pile became "critical" (i.e. the chain reaction was just sustained). By pulling out the control rod a little bit more, power was produced.

Smooth control of a reactor depends upon the fact that some of the fission neutrons do not come out promptly. If they all did, the power of the reactor would increase 160,000 times in one minute. Some neutrons are delayed, and the power is actually less than doubled in one minute. This gives plenty of time to operate the control rods. It is, in fact, impossible for a properly designed reactor to go off like a bomb.

Today there are many different kinds of nuclear reactors using various kinds of fuel—natural uranium, separated uranium-235, uranium + thorium, and uranium + plutonium, are some examples. Different moderators are used too—ordinary water, HEAVY WATER, graphite, and beryllium are among them. New control methods are needed for today's reactors. But these reactors work in much the same way as the first one under the stadium—it is just like the difference between a Model-T Ford and a new Lincoln. They both work, but one works better than the other.

11

Why Atomic Energy Is Safe

Atomic Energy means anything to do with the breaking up of atomic nuclei. A nuclear power station works on atomic energy, and so does the dial of a watch that glows in the dark.

When radioactivity was first discovered people did not know how dangerous it could be. The Curies discovered radium by crystallizing radium salts in rows of dishes, handling them with bare hands, and radiologists who used the first X–ray machines used to test them by taking pictures of their own bones. Years later many of these pioneers died because of the radiation their bodies had absorbed. They were not stupid—they just did not know how dangerous radiation could be.

Today the effects of radiation are better understood than most of the other risks that man has to face. An International Commission on Radiological

Protection (ICRP) sets limits on the amount of radiation permitted for people and the International Atomic Energy Agency (IAEA) gives practical advice on how the recommendations of the ICRP can be carried out. Most countries have their own national regulations but all are based on the ICRP recommendations and most of them accept the advice of the IAEA. The details of atomic energy regulations vary from one country to another, but the important parts are all about the same.

In most countries a government agency draws up national regulations and sees that they are carried out. It also issues licenses for operation of isotope laboratories, nuclear power stations, and radioactive devices used in industry.

When a large nuclear enterprise like an atomic power station or fuel REPROCESSING factory is proposed, the agency carries out a very complete examination of the design. It insists on an automatic safety system which will shut operations down as soon as any trouble develops, and a "containment" system (such as a concrete dome or steel shell) which will prevent radioactivity from leaving the building if a serious accident does happen.

To make sure of the safety of the plant the designer usually has to imagine the worst accident that could possibly occur. He must then suppose that the automatic shut-down devices *do not work.* He must satisfy the agency that if all this happens at a time when the weather would produce the worst pollution problems *no member of the public will be hurt.* This is as if the designer of a jet aircraft had to prove that if the plane full of passengers fell in Times Square nobody would be hurt.

Radioactivity is dangerous if it is not handled properly, yet nuclear industry has a first-class safety record. Radiation cannot be detected by sight, sound, smell or touch, and very powerful sources of radiation are used every day by thousands of people. Why aren't they hurt?

It is not much use having good rules if we do not carry them out. Fortunately a great deal is known about how to avoid RADIATION HAZARDS. People called "health physicists" are trained in the science of Radiation Safety and it is their job to see that the radiation dose of workers and the public is kept well below the legal limit.

There are three important ways to protect against radiation. For short, they are called "shielding," "distance" and "time."

Shielding

We saw in Chapter 1 that α rays are stopped by paper, β rays by a thin metal sheet, and γ rays by thick lead blocks. A man who is working with a substance that emits α or β particles is safe if he has a piece of transparent plastic between him and the source. Some β particles have more energy than others so the thickness of the sheet will depend on what isotope he is working with. The γ rays also have various energies, but for the kind of quantities used in laboratories a few inches of lead is enough to protect the worker. A nuclear reactor, of course, contains so much more activity that many feet of concrete shielding is built around the core. The type of shielding is chosen to suit the source of

radiation, so no matter how powerful the source is, only a fraction of the radiation can get through.

Distance

Sometimes it is impossible to use enough shielding to stop the radiation sufficiently. Then we have to move away from the source. Everybody knows that as you step back from a fire the heat drops off very quickly. It is the same with nuclear radiation. If you go twice as far away you only receive a *quarter* of the dose (not half, as you might expect!).

If you have to stand a long distance from your work you need special tools. These may simply be long tongs for picking up apparatus or taking out stoppers, or they may be very clever and expensive devices which act as mechanical arms and hands. These REMOTE CONTROL MECHANISMS look terribly complicated, but they are easy to use. There is a little device at one end for the operator's hand. At the other end are claws that move exactly as the operator moves his fingers and the mechanical hand twists as he twists his wrist and moves around in exact time with his hand when the operator moves his arm. All this is done by a system of springs, pulleys, and sometimes small electric motors. A person using a remote control device for the first time is always amazed—in a few minutes

he forgets he is using a tool and carries on just as if the claws were his own hands even though they may be several feet away behind a thick shielding window!

Time

If you only spend half the time in a radiation field you will only get half the dose of radiation. This is so simple that it seems silly to mention it, but health physicists and radiation workers have to remind themselves about it all the time. In an atomic energy plant the radiation field will be different in different places. In the offices and most of the laboratories it will be about at the level of "natural background" but in some places it will be much higher.

The health physicist puts up a radiation danger sign in such places, and a notice giving the radiation field. The foreman can tell from the notice how long he can allow a man to work in that place and still receive less than his allowable dose of radiation.

Protective Clothing

Shielding, distance, and time, can be very effective in protecting workers, particularly from direct radiation. However INTERNAL contamination can be more dangerous and less easy to pre-

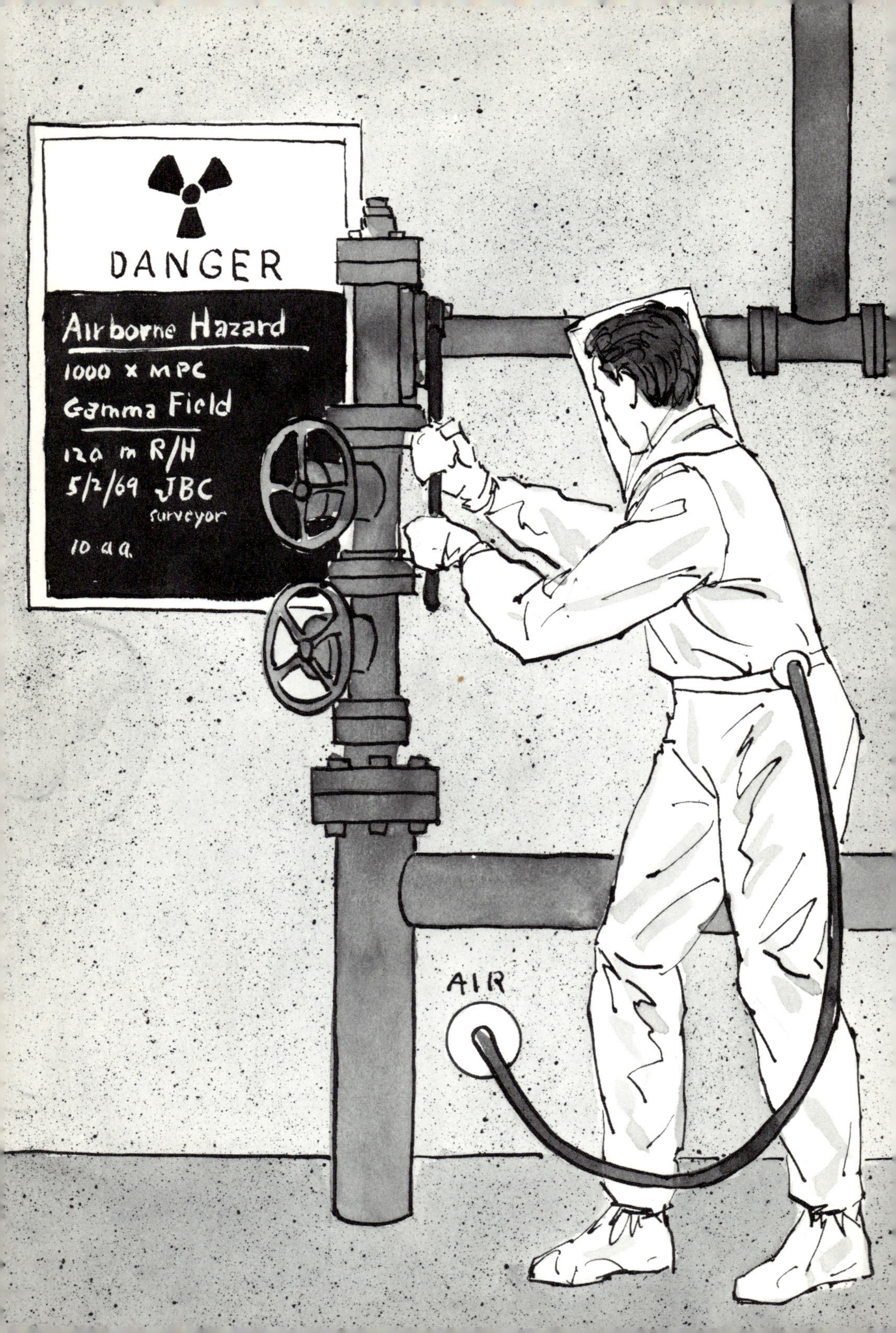
DANGER
Airborne Hazard
1000 x MPC
Gamma Field
120 m R/H
5/2/69 JBC
surveyor
10 a.a.
AIR

vent. Breathing air contaminated by radioactive dusts and absorbing radioactive material by mouth or through the skin, would give us a personal BODY BURDEN of radiation that we would carry around with us and which sometimes could stay with us for a long time.

People who work with radioactivity wear rubber gloves which they change when they become contaminated. They also wear protective clothing. This may be an ordinary lab coat or coveralls. Special rubbers or boots may be needed, and if the air is polluted a gas mask may have to be worn. In the most contaminated areas the workers may look almost like deep-sea divers, sealed up from head to foot inside a plastic suit, with fresh air lines for cooling the suit as well as for breathing. The more protective clothing you have the clumsier you are likely to be, so everything is done to keep contamination at the lowest possible level.

Ventilation

A good way to prevent breathing of contaminated air is to remove it. Atomic energy plants must have a good ventilation system and a sensible layout. Clean air enters at the "clean" end of the plant, and it leaves at the "dirty" end. This prevents air being carried from radioactive areas. Laboratory work is usually done in fume hoods with a strong current of air being drawn from the room into the hood. Air movement is checked by smoke generators because even the best designers sometimes find that the air does not move the way they expected, especially if a door is left open that they supposed would be kept shut.

Air coming from the ventilation system may, of course, be contaminated. Before it goes up the stack to the open air it passes through filters which remove the finest dust particles. If there is radioactive iodine in the air it is removed by a special filter packed with charcoal.

Monitoring

The health physicist must always remember Murphy's Law. This says "If something can go wrong, sooner or later it will." All the precautions must be constantly checked to see that they are working, and workers must be checked to be sure that they are really receiving less than the permitted dose of radiation. This checking is called MONITORING.

Radiation workers wear a "photo-badge" containing a piece of photographic film. This is blackened by radiation and the amount of blackening is a measure of radiation dose. Workers in the more active areas wear "pencil chambers"—some

of these record the dose on a tiny dial and others sound a buzzer when a pre-set dose is reached.

When people leave a laboratory they monitor their hands, feet, and clothing with Geiger counters, and there is often an alarm at the gate to catch the contaminated person who has somehow passed through all the checks. There are change rooms with showers and sprays in the more active areas, where workers make a complete change of clothing before leaving, and they are carefully monitored as they leave in their street clothes.

Inside the plant, health physicists are constantly on the move with counters checking surfaces such as floors and bench tops, and if they find any contamination it is cleaned up by DECONTAMINATION OPERATORS. They have an important job because one of the best ways to spread contamination is to track it around on the feet. Remember that the dose of radiation permitted for each worker is very small and it is *all on the record.* A contaminated plant will just stop operating if it is not cleaned up.

Strict regulations, recording of exposure, efficient monitoring, and the network of safety devices all work together to make nuclear industry as safe as it has proved to be.

12

Present and Future

What does "nuclear industry" amount to today? Is it really big, like General Motors, or quite a small affair like the local paint and body shop? Are we talking about an industry that affects the lives of millions of people, or just a few hundred scientists and technicians spending public money on a dream?

Nuclear industry *is* big—not as big as General Motors, but it does affect the lives of millions of people. We will look at nuclear power first, because that is the part of the industry that makes most of the headlines.

NUCLEAR POWER. About half the new electric power stations built in 1968 in the United States were atomic power stations, and the figure was higher in Britain. In five years' time, in the mid-1970's, three-quarters of new American power stations will be nuclear. Why is this happening? What makes people want nuclear power?

To generate electricity you need a source of energy. This may be water power from a natural cataract like Niagara Falls or a big dam like Bonneville or Hoover. Or it may be a furnace burning coal or oil or gas. The water, or the steam produced by the heat of the furnace, turns the turbine that generates the electricity. In an atomic power station the "furnace" is the nuclear reactor. It is the source of the heat, and the rest of the station is similar to any plant fired by gas or oil or coal.

Ordinary fuels are called "fossil fuels" because they were formed millions of years ago from living creatures—plants or animals. The source of energy for these forms of life was the sun, so when we burn fossil fuels today we are really using the energy of the sun that shone on the earth millions of years ago. When we "burn" uranium in a reactor we are using a much older source of energy. It is the energy that went into the making of the uranium atoms, and nobody really understands yet how it worked, or where it came from, but we do know how to use it.

When we burn fossil fuel, part of it goes up the smoke stack, and with coal a great deal is left behind as ash. The stack gases contain carbon monoxide, sulfur dioxide and often various organic compounds, as well as solid particles (soot and "fly ash") that settle out on the ground. Good filters can remove most of the particles and very high stacks help to dilute the gases into a lot of air, but the best of fossil fuel furnaces cause at least some pollution.

We do not really burn uranium. The fission reaction splits the uranium atom, forming fission products and a lot of heat. But the fission products do not go up the stack—they stay in the fuel elements. The uranium is sealed inside a jacket made of stainless steel or ZIRCONIUM, and it stays there until the fuel is unloaded from the reactor and taken to a re-processing plant.

Sometimes the cladding around the uranium may puncture, or a weld may be badly made (remember Murphy's Law?). This does not happen very often—if it did the station would shut itself down automatically. But to protect the public, filters are put into the ventilating air that goes up the stack. The system is so efficient that some of the latest nuclear power stations do not have a tall stack and yet they have been able to satisfy safety boards that the public is in no danger.

Now that people understand the effects of pollution, nuclear stations are popular because they are "clean." However, so are hydro stations—the ones driven by water power. These are also very cheap to run, although the dams are expensive to build. The trouble with hydro power is that we are running out of sites in North America. To find a good "fall" or "head" of water you must go far into the wilderness, and bringing electricity hundreds of miles by cable is very costly. If power from Churchill Falls in Labrador was brought to New York, it would cost about five times as much in New York as it did in Labrador. Nuclear power stations can now be built quite near big cities, so the cost of transmitting the electricity is saved.

A few tons of uranium can produce as much power as a mountain of coal or many shiploads of oil. Transportation costs for nuclear fuel are therefore very low. This can be the deciding reason for "going nuclear" if the site is far from a port or a coalfield.

The cost of power from nuclear stations has come down so quickly during the last few years that in most places it is no more than we would have to pay for fossil fuel power. This is a very new industry, and we can expect the costs to continue to come down. When we add together cheapness and convenience and freedom from pollution, we can see why nuclear power can now compete with fossil fuel power.

MEDICAL USES. Long before most people thought of nuclear power as a practical possibility, they were talking about the "cobalt bomb." This is not a bomb at all—it is simply a very intense source of COBALT-60 inside a thick box made of lead or uranium. The box is a shield, which prevents any of the powerful cobalt-60 γ rays from escaping. A hole in the box can be opened by a mechanical shutter arrangement so that a thin pencil of gamma rays can be turned in any direction by turning the box.

Cobalt-60 radiation is better than X-rays for many purposes, including treatment of cancers deep in the body. X-rays give a much larger dose of radiation to the skin and to normal tissues near the surface. This, of course, is not wanted if the cancer is deeper in the body. The colbalt-60 γ rays liberate more of their energy where it is needed.

Hundreds of thousands of CURIES of cobalt-60 go into these TELETHERAPY machines every year. The demand for this isotope of cobalt is so great that some power reactors are now putting cobalt into their control rods instead of cadmium or some other neutron absorber. When the control rods are changed the cobalt-60 is extracted.

Some diseases can be treated by injecting a radioactive isotope into the bloodstream. This is because some elements are concentrated in certain organs of the body. For example, iodine is picked up very quickly by the THYROID GLAND. If a person has an over-active thyroid and he is injected with radioactive iodine (iodine-131) the isotope will concentrate in the gland and it will receive a very high dose of radiation. This is much better than giving a dose of radiation from the outside, which might damage surrounding normal tissues.

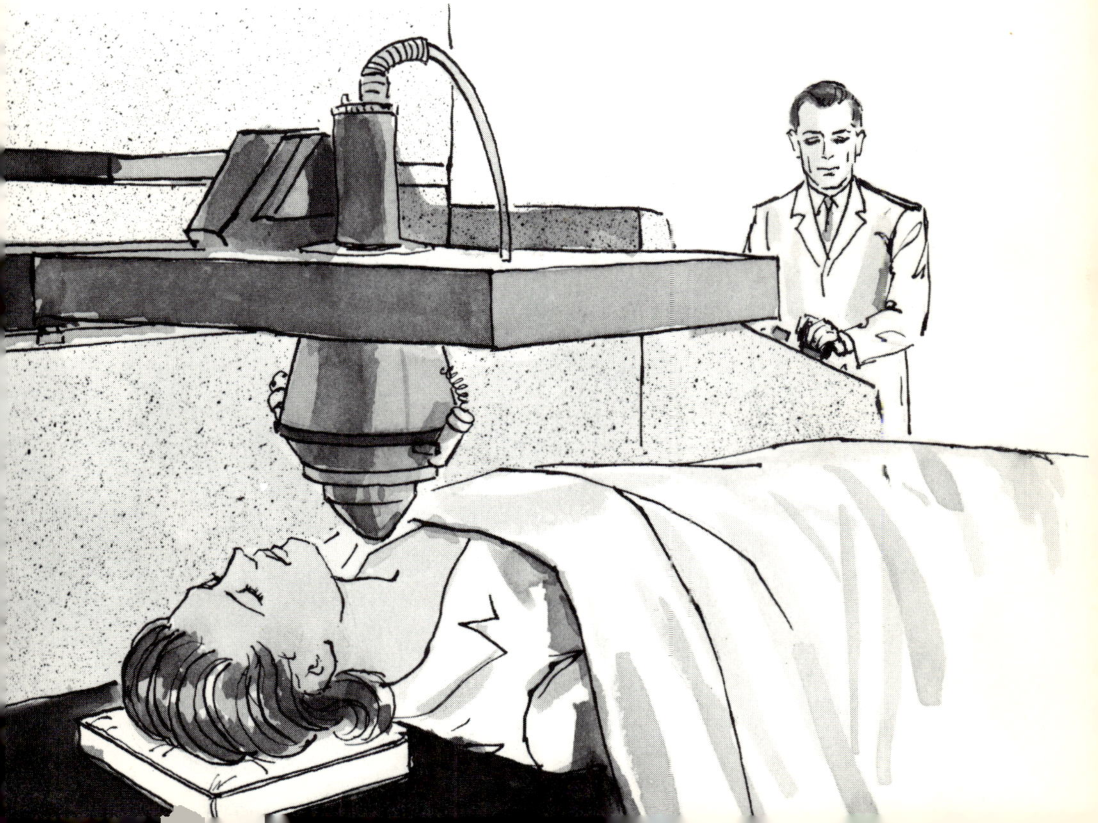

Radioactive isotopes are useful in diagnosis as well as treatment. A thyroid cancer can be found by giving a very small dose of iodine-131. A counter is passed over the gland and the position of the cancer is shown by a large number of counts. This is done by a machine called a "scanner." The counter is shielded so that it "sees" only a small area of the patient's neck. It moves slowly across the neck and the counts are printed out on paper as lines or dots. It does this over the whole area of the thyroid gland, so the doctor gets a picture showing the position of the cancer as a dark patch—where there are many marks there was a high count.

Similar methods can be used for diagnosing tumors of the brain, spleen, liver, lungs, pancreas and other organs, using various different isotopes that concentrate in these organs. Sometimes the cancer does not pick up the isotope, but the normal organ does. Then the cancer appears on the scan as a light patch.

Isotopes are also useful in medicine as "tracers." In some diseases it is useful to know the *circulation time* of the blood—how long it takes for the blood to go around the body. If a little blood is taken and some radioactive chromium is added, the chromium attaches itself to the red blood cells. If this "labelled" blood is injected into an arm vein, for instance, a counter put over the other arm or a leg will give a big increase in counting rate when the labelled blood passes beneath it. The time taken for the labelled blood to go from the injection site to the counter is a measure of the circulation time.

Red blood cells labelled with radioactive chromium can also be used to find out how much blood there is in a patient's body. This is a bit harder to explain, but we will try because the idea behind it is used in many fields besides medicine.

Imagine that you have 1/20 of a pint of blood with the red cells labelled with enough radioactive chromium for a counter to register 10,000 counts per minute. You inject this blood into an arm vein and wait for a few minutes until the blood has travelled around so many times that it is well mixed with all the rest of the blood in the body. Then you take out the same amount of blood from a vein and find that the counting rate is 50 counts per minute. Evidently the blood you injected has been diluted by the blood in the body from 10,000 counts down to 50 counts—200 times. So the body must contain 200 times as much blood as the amount (1/20 pint) that you injected. Since 200 × 1/20 is 10, the body contains 10 pints of blood.

There are so many ways that radioisotopes can be used in medicine that large hospitals often have an Isotope Department. Many advances in medical research, as well as diagnosis and treatment, have been made, using this new tool of science.

AGRICULTURE. Most farmers work out their own problems and one would not expect radioactivity to be much use on a farm. But what if a man wants to know if it is better to put fertilizer right on the row, just alongside the row, or in the middle between rows? He can try it, and wait a whole season to see the effects, but it is better to leave this sort of question to a research station.

Fertilizers can be mixed with radioactive ingredients. They can be put on the soil or sprayed on the crop (many fertilizers go in through the leaves very well). Then the amount of radioactivity in the plants will show just how much fertilizer went where it was supposed to go. The crop can be taken at different times during the season to see if the fertilizer is still being taken up, and you can even see just where it goes inside the plant by "counting" the roots, stems, leaves, or flowers.

Animals have diseases as well as men, and veterinary medicine uses isotopes too. There is one success story that started with the veterinarians and opened up new uses for radioactivity. Cattlemen suffer big losses, and the cattle suffer too, from the "screw worm fly." They lay their eggs under the skin of the cattle and when the grubs hatch out they make horrible sores which become infected and are very painful. Scientists found that the female screw worm fly—like many other insects—only mates once in its life. So they gave some male flies a large dose of radiation (from cobalt-60). This was not enough to kill them, or to stop them from mating, but it did make them sterile. When a sterile male mated with a female, she laid eggs that did not hatch.

The scientists then went to the island of Curaçao, where screw worm trouble was very bad, taking with them thousands of irradiated flies. They released the flies to mate with the native female flies, producing sterile eggs. Very soon there was not a screw worm fly left on the island. It turned out that you do not have to have an island—flies only travel short distances. So this method is being used in many other places, and with many other insects.

INDUSTRY. Radioactivity is so important in industry that several years ago it was said that radioisotopes had saved industry $500 million in one year.

X-rays are used to find faults in metal work such as pipes and boilers. Cobalt-60 and IRIDIUM-192

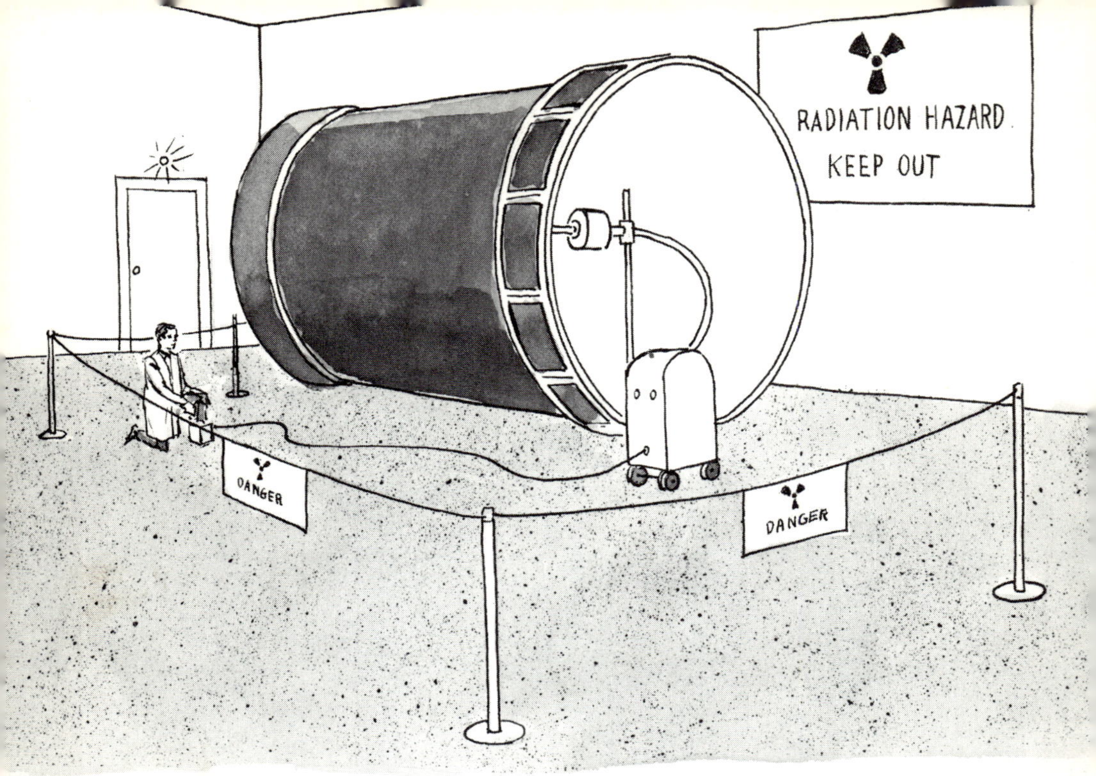

are more convenient because they need no electric power, emit very penetrating radiation, and can be put in places too awkward for an X-ray source. The isotope is placed on one side of the metal and a photographic film on the other. If there is a fault in a weld or a crack in the metal it shows up as a dark line on the developed film.

Wear on moving metal parts can be detected by plating the part with some radioactive material. The radioactivity is rubbed off and appears in the oil, or the worn part can be covered with a photographic film which will be blackened at the places that are less worn.

The thickness of sheets of metal or paper can be gauged by having a radioactive isotope under the sheet and a counter above it. As the sheet is moved the counter will show increased counts at thin spots. This is very important in paper mills where the paper travels at high speed. If the machinery is not working properly, thin and thick patches make the paper useless. The counting rates are fed into a computer which automatically adjusts the machine.

When a sewer pipe breaks it is often hard to find out just where the break is. If a radioactive isotope is put into the sewer it will leak out through the break and the patch of activity can be found by passing a counter over the ground.

Different kinds of oil are often sent down one pipeline and the people at the refinery want to know when the next batch is arriving. If the first portion of the new lot is radioactive it is easy to detect.

The killing power of radioactivity is being used to sterilize surgical instruments and reduce spoilage of foods by bacteria and molds. Cobalt-60 is used for this in very large amounts. Smaller sources are used to give a sufficient radiation dose to potatoes, carrots and onions to prevent sprouting during storage.

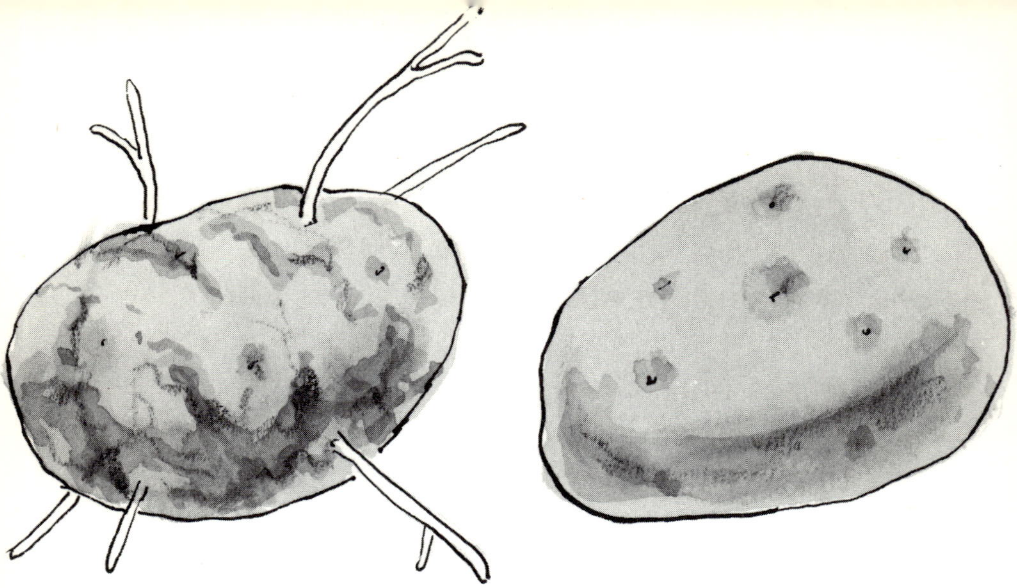

Nuclear power usually comes in large amounts —from power stations—but some very small power plants work on radioisotopes. Remember that radium is always warm, and so is any isotope that is decaying. A source of heat is a source of power and sometimes we need a small power source that will go on producing electricity for a long time—longer than the lifetime of the best battery. Strontium-90 has a half-life of 30 years, and it can be made into a substance (strontium titanate) which is very hard and will not dissolve in water. Isotopes like this can be used to provide power for ocean buoys, space ships, artificial hearts, watches and the beeping boxes that sit on the sea bed to give SONAR signals from submarines.

Chemists have known for a long time that heat affects chemical reactions and they soon discovered that nuclear radiation could break up large molecules. Later on they found that radiation helps some large molecules to join together. Shrink-proof and permanent-crease cloths contain man-made fibers, and some of these could not be produced without the help of intense radiation.

These are only a few of the more common uses for radioisotopes in industry. We will finish with something you may have in your own home—a static eliminator. Some phonograph pick-up heads carry a little device which removes dust from in front of the needle. This often contains a tiny source of POLONIUM. The radiation ionizes the air, which discharges the electric charge on the dust. It is this charge that makes the dust stick to the record. In industry "static electricity" is a great nuisance, particularly in textile mills, and radioisotopes help to control it.

THE FUTURE

Predicting the future is dangerous—it usually turns out to be different from the forecast and sometimes is more astonishing. Some things are clearly coming up so we will stick to them.

BREEDER REACTORS are just around the corner. When uranium is bombarded with neutrons it is only the U-235 isotope that splits up and produces the heat and fission products. The remaining 99.3 percent of the uranium (U-238) absorbs neutrons and forms plutonium. Now plutonium is FISSILE—it splits up like U-235, producing heat. You cannot get the full power out of the reactor by leaving the fuel in until all the plutonium has disappeared, because the fission products absorb too many neutrons. However, you can separate the plutonium by reprocessing and use it as a fuel—a fuel that has been "bred" in the reactor. Thorium, too, breeds another fissile fuel, uranium-233. Reactors are being designed and tested to use plutonium and U-233 as fuels. This is important because we shall be able to use more of the energy in fuel than is possible today—this will economize on uranium.

Up to now nuclear power plants have been too expensive for use in commercial transportation, though they are used in naval vessels. Improvements will certainly lead to more efficient nuclear ships. The problem in land or air transportation is the weight of the shielding needed around the reactor, but some kinds of rockets are likely to be driven by nuclear power. They will be well out in space before the reactor is dangerously radioactive, so no shielding will be needed.

"Fusion" is a subject we have not mentioned before. This is what happens in the hydrogen bomb. Deuterium is an isotope of hydrogen with double the normal atomic weight. If two deuterium atoms join together (fuse) they produce an enormous outburst of energy, but they will only do this at a very high temperature—about as hot as the sun. This kind of temperature occurs in an atomic explosion, but a *controlled* temperature like this cannot be reached in a furnace. It would melt the furnace.

Scientists have produced these temperatures for a fraction of a second in a special device called a TORUS. Very strong magnets are arranged around a tube carrying a stream of charged deuterium atoms. The magnetic field squeezes the stream tightly together, raising the temperature, and at the same time keeps the hot gas away from the tube. The big problem is to keep the reaction going, and to produce more power from the reaction than you use up in driving the magnets. One day this may be solved, and then we shall have "clean" power with no fission products and no need to mine uranium. All the deuterium we need can be found in the sea in the form of heavy water.

These are developments that are in the laboratories or on the drawing boards now. Some of them may be in action even before you read this book. But there will be other discoveries, perhaps unthought of today—this is a very fast-moving science. When I was at school in the 1920's some people thought that physics was just about at the end of big discoveries, and now there are those who wonder if atomic energy is near the end of the road. Well, just look what happened to physics since the 1920's!

Glossary

BARIUM A rather heavy metal resembling calcium.

BERYLLIUM-RADON SOURCE Beryllium, a very light metal found in the semi-precious stone beryl, gives out neutrons when hit by the α rays from radium. Anything that emits radiation is called a "source."

BISMUTH A light metal best known as a constituent of "upset stomach" remedies.

BODY BURDEN The amount of radioactive material inside a person's body is called the "body burden." Regulations set the "maximum permissible body burden." Atomic energy workers must keep their body burden below this level.

BREEDER REACTORS Breeder reactors are so called because they form more fissile material than they consume. This is not really an example of "perpetual motion" because non-fissile uranium-238 is used up in the process.

CLADDING The uranium fuel in a reactor is enclosed in a can made of a non-corrodible metal. This protects the fuel and also prevents fission products from entering the coolant.

CLOUD CHAMBER DEVICE If radiation passes through a saturated vapor, the vapor condenses on the ionized air. This forms a visible track which can be photographed. The "contrails" of jet aircraft are somewhat like this.

COBALT-60 A radioactive isotope of the metal, cobalt. Cobalt occurs along with nickel or silver in ores. It is used in making stainless steel and blue or green pigments. It also occurs in the vitamin necessary for prevention of pernicious anemia!

CONDUCTOR — Conductors for electricity are usually made of copper wire. Air is usually a good insulator, but air around radioactive material conducts electricity quite well.

CRITICALITY — Criticality is the condition of being "critical." If a reactor is critical it is producing just enough neutrons to keep the chain reaction going. Increasing the neutron supply increases the power output very quickly.

CURIES — The Curie is the unit of measurement of radioactivity, just as the pound is a unit of measurement of weight. It is written with a capital letter because it is named in honor of Marie Curie.

DECAY All radioactive elements decay. This breakup of the atoms is the cause of the radioactivity. However some decay very quickly—half of the atoms of iodine-139 break up in 2 seconds—but it takes 16 million *years* for half the atoms of iodine-129 to decay.

DECONTAMINATION OPERATORS People who remove radioactive contamination from equipment, instruments and buildings by washing, scrubbing, soaking in solvents and other methods such as supersonic cleaning (i.e. treatment with high-frequency sound, which is very efficient in knocking dirt off anything).

DENSITY Density is measured by weight per unit volume. A pound of a very dense material like lead is a small object compared with a pound of Styrofoam, which has a very low density.

ELECTRON An electron is a single charge

of negative electricity. It has almost no weight, and can move very fast. A current of electricity is a stream of electrons.

FISSILE When the atoms of certain elements are hit by a neutron they break up. If more than one neutron comes out during the breakup a chain reaction is possible. Such elements are "fissile." Examples are uranium-235, uranium-233 and plutonium-239.

FLUORINE A gas which is normally found combined in substances called fluorides. It is also used in making plastics and the cooling gas in many refrigerators.

FUSE "Fuse" usually means "melt," but to atomic scientists it means the joining together of two atoms to make a new kind of atom.

GEIGER COUNTER This works rather like an electroscope. An electrically charged rod is held by an insulator inside a metal tube connected to the ground. If the gas inside the tube is made a conductor by radiation, a pulse of electricity runs through the gas to the ground. These pulses go through an amplifier which is connected to the recording device or to earphones. The number of pulses per minute is a measure of the radioactivity.

GRAM — A unit of weight in the metric system. 1000 grams is about 2 pounds.

GRAPHITE — A form of carbon. Charcoal is carbon in a non-crystalline form. Diamond is carbon in large crystals. Graphite has very small flat crystals. It is used for making pencils and lubricants.

HEAVY WATER — Ordinary water molecules consist of two hydrogen atoms combined with one oxygen atom. Heavy water molecules contain two deuterium atoms and one oxygen atom. Deuterium is an isotope of hydrogen. The deuterium atom is twice as heavy as an ordinary hydrogen atom. Natural water contains a very small amount of heavy water.

HELIUM One of the "noble" or "rare" gases. They occur in small amounts in air but helium sometimes occurs in large amounts in natural gas. It is used for filling balloons and (since liquid helium is the coldest substance known) for refrigeration. Other noble gases are argon, neon, krypton, xenon, radon and thoron.

INTERNAL This means "inside the body." Different elements go to different parts of the body. Strontium, for example, goes to bone but cesium spreads all over the body. Zinc is found in the white blood cells.

IONIZED — The molecules of a gas are usually not electrically charged. However if some kind of radiation passes through the gas an electron may be knocked out of an atom, leaving the molecule with a positive electric charge. It is then said to be "ionized" and the charged gas molecule is an "ion."

IRIDIUM-192 — A radioactive isotope of iridium, which is a precious metal resembling platinum.

ISOTOPES — All elements can be obtained in various forms. For example ordinary hydrogen atoms weigh 1 unit, but there are two other forms of hydrogen. One, "deuterium" weighs 2 units, and the other, "tritium" weighs 3 units. Atoms having the same chemical properties but different weights are called *isotopes*. Some isotopes (e.g. tritium) are radioactive but others (e.g. hydrogen and deuterium) are not.

MODERATOR Any substance that slows down neutrons is a moderator. Examples are graphite, beryllium (a light metal) and heavy water.

MONITORING Checking with a measuring instrument. A "monitor" is a man who uses some kind of instrument (such as a Geiger counter) to measure radiation.

NUCLEUS The central part of the atom, containing very nearly all the weight.

PENETRATING Refers to passing through matter. Gamma rays are usually penetrating, but alpha particles are not.

PHOSPHORESCENT Literally, "shines in the dark." Phosphorescent substances shine after the "exciting radiation" (light, X-rays etc.) has stopped; fluorescent" substances only shine while the exciting radiation is present (e.g. fluorescent paint).

POLONIUM — A natural radioisotope discovered by Marie Curie during her isolation of radium from pitchblende.

PROTON — A single positive charge of electricity. Protons are much heavier than electrons. The nucleus of the atom is made up of protons and neutrons.

RADIATION HAZARDS — A "hazard" is a risk. It is not exactly a danger. It is only dangerous if you do not take the proper precautions.

RADIATION SHIELD — An object through which radiation will not pass. For example, people working with radioactive material often protect themselves with a wall of lead bricks.

RADIOACTIVE ISOTOPE — There are several isotopes of every element. Some are radioactive and some are not —the latter are "stable" isotopes. For example, sulfur has

4 stable isotopes and 4 radioactive ones.

RADIUM Radium is a very rare radioactive element, used mainly for medical purposes and for making luminous paints. It is everywhere in slight traces which can be detected by delicate instruments. In the same way there are tiny traces of gold everywhere which can be measured by modern devices, even though there is not enough to separate it out at a reasonable cost.

RARE EARTH A group of elements that chemists found very difficult to separate. We now know how to do it, and some of them have turned out not to be so rare after all. Cerium, for example, makes the sparks in automatic lighters and several rare earth elements are used in producing color in television sets.

REMOTE CONTROL MECHANISM Any device (such as a pair of tongs) that enables you to operate at a distance is a remote control mechanism, but this usually means a complicated system of levers and springs that will serve to pick up a bottle, remove the cap, empty the bottle and replace the cap at a distance of several feet and on the other side of a shielding wall.

REPROCESSING When the fuel is removed from a nuclear reactor it still contains some unchanged uranium, some plutonium and also fission products. The uranium and plutonium are valuable and must be recovered. The fuel is dissolved in acid and the uranium and plutonium are extracted, leaving the fission products behind as radioactive waste. The place where this is done is a "reprocessing plant."

SONAR Sound travels well through water. If a box producing "beeps" is on the bottom of the sea the beeps can be heard far away by a listening device. The sound waves will be reflected from a submarine and thus give the position of the submarine by a system worked on the same principle as radar. The sound detection system is called "sonar."

TELETHERAPY Literally "curing at a distance." The cobalt-60 inside its shield is several inches away from the patient and only the gamma rays touch his body.

THYROID GLAND The thyroid is a gland in the neck which controls the rate at which energy is produced in the body.

TRANSMUTATION Men have always wanted to be able to change one metal into another; for example, mercury into gold or lead into silver. This is what the alchemists tried to do by a mixture of chemistry and magic. They called the art "transmutation."

TORUS A tube bent round into a ring.

X-RAYS When a stream of electrons hits a sheet of metal, a very penetrating radiation is produced called X-rays or Roentgen rays. They are similar to gamma rays and are used in medicine and industry for similar purposes.

ZIRCONIUM A metal that does not corrode in hot water and can be made into strong pipes and even boilers. It absorbs fewer neutrons than most other metals, so it is useful in nuclear reactors.

Index

Page numbers in italics refer to Glossary entries.